Discovery

Bianca Sanders

Copyright © 2015 Bianca Sanders

All rights reserved.

ISBN: **0692357262**

ISBN-13: **978-0692357262**

DEDICATION

To the man that brought color to the grey. To Zephaniah and Zechariah, Thank you for showing me that there is such a thing as loving in permanent.

CONTENTS

Acknowledgments

Over and Over
Nothing Permanent
Road Trippin'
Instincts: Free Write
Touch
Don't Trust: Free Write
Irreplaceable
If It's Any Consolation
You to You
Optimism
Choices
Grateful For It All: Free Write
Leave the Door Unlocked/3 AM
Last Mistake
Hopeful
Blue Skies
Charlie
Discovery
Night Falls
A Poem for Joseph
The Boy
Mental Disorder
Movement
Art to Another Artist
Reminisce
Still
Lost
A Poem to My Boys
Where To
15 Is Not Enough
Little Things
I Never
Just Waiting
Sobering
Start Over
Final Explanation
Feel
Long Walk
In Time
More Than This
Conversations With Lois
Penetration
Somtime-y

Bianca Sanders

Words That Lost The Meaning
Habits
More Than I Can Bare
Never Again
Doing It Wrong
The Longest Wait Ever
The Count Of Monte Cristo
The Letter

ACKNOWLEDGMENTS

I want to thank everyone who find themselves in my insanity. It's nice to know I am not alone. To the distance that changed us, bring us back, full circle stronger than before.

Over and Over

I want that sex on a rooftop
Quiet the boys are sleeping
Orgasms' at 100 mph
I don't have to tell him
He already knows what to do with it
6 shots of Patrón
Cause he said so
Speak life into your piece
You taste so sweet
Forget about yesterday
I can't promise you tomorrow
But I'll bind you to my bedroom
Leave scratches down your back
Bruises on your thighs
And my scent on your skin
Baby I promise
You'll want this
Over
And over
Again

NOTHING PERMANENT

There are often so many tragedies in what should be love
More often than not
I fall in love with people who are
Unavailable
They are usually in love with their ex's
Or their jobs
Or hobbies
Or if I'm lucky all of the above
I meet them, get to know them and touch them knowing that eventually there will be no wedding
Nothing beautiful or harmonious to celebrate
Just a drawn out funeral for everything I knew we never would be
I date men more broken than I could ever be
So as to not make my inner feminist upset
I choke on words like "I love you" and I only apologize when I don't mean it
So as to not confuse my inner demons
See the truth is
It's not them it's me
I actually enjoy being alone

I just crave temporary company.
I don't fear losing people the way I fear losing feelings
I hate memories
They are the worst kind of wound

ROAD TRIPPIN'

I say I just want to get away
Light-years from this place
My heart is heavy with the idea of traveling alone
But I think subconsciously
I prefer it this way
Going 80 down the highway
Wind through my hair
Sun in my eyes
No traffic
Open to the possibility of anything
This is where I was meant to be
This is how I know
I'm living

INSTINCT: FREE WRITE

Always trust your instinct. People often lie or try to steer you in a direction they want for you or what they would choose for themselves. Not always out of negativity or with malicious intent but because they can (or believe they can) see what you can't. But your programming won't steer you wrong. The actual definition of 'instinct'(according to Webster) is: "an innate typically fixed pattern of behavior in animals in response to certain stimuli" .Your 'response to certain stimuli' may be very different from what the next person's response would be. I am not saying don't seek advice. I am not saying don't weigh all your options. I am saying, that in order to come to a conclusion that you see fit. Trust your own programming. Whether, it's relationships or everyday activities your brain and body will respond according to you and nothing else. People will often lie to one another and try to lie to themselves even but their instinct will always know the difference.

TOUCH

He touched me in ways that made my river run wild
He cradled my inner beast so softly
She tamed just for him
Purring in his mouth trading energy for love songs
And I'm so sensitive
So he's gentle
I crave him in large doses
Penetrate my membrane
Make me think
Lost in his ways
Adaptation touch the frame
And then he breathes
Life into me
A creation of us both
He left his fingerprints
Not just on my body
But on my soul
He is the last man to ever touch me

This love is just for him

DON'T TRUST: FREE WRITE GONE POEM

Sometimes you push people away
Not because you don't want them
Or want them to phase out
But because you are either not ready
Or searching for something more
More along the lines of deep conversations and a full understanding of how they work and what they need
Sometimes you need them to make you hit your peak as a person and not just sexually
What's it matter if you're perfect in the bedroom and can do nothing outside of it.
Always searching for the next great thing instead of what you have.
I have found that investing in other people is probably the most dangerous thing you can do.
Not because they lie and/or hurt you
Even though people often do
But because you are volunteering a power over you that will be hard to retrieve
Never subject yourself to open fire IF the person wielding the

weapon can't be trusted
Sometimes people hurt you because they are not in touch with what they want
But if you are in tune with yourself you should be able to sense this
You can tell when they are holding your time and emotions hostage until they decide what they want.
These are the most selfish of people
Do not let your guard down around them
Trust your instinct
Your intuition
Your judgement
People's mouths often lie
But their actions and heart rarely do
There's no science to the madness
Just ways to lessen the blow
So yes, she probably wants you
Ye, you're probably more than pink matter to him
The walls come down
The guards are called off and they have shown you who they really are
Don't argue with what you see
But dispute what you've been told

IRREPLACEABLE

Everybody wants a spot that's not theirs.
It's his.
It seems
As
If
I should let you have that seat
It's appears to be so simple to all of you.
But there's something to be said of appearances.
They hold very little value.
I'm not trying to be rude.
You'd probably make for better conversation.
But he was here long before I even knew he existed.
Took up space in my dreams
Before I even knew what his hands looked like
He touched me.
You think you want to take his place
But you don't know what that takes.
Because I am not easy to handle
And I don't make for good conversation these days
My mind is still in another place.

A want vs a need
They aren't the same.
I've drifted down the rabbit hole
You'll have to wait if you're trying to stay.
It's not about who is better.
It's about who makes you hear the music
Who makes the colors pop
Who make the words show up on paper
Who makes the noise quiet down
Who makes the chaos make sense
Who makes you believe that you can overcome anything
That anything is possible.
I'm not saying that you can't.
I'm saying I'd rather that he does it.
I need time.
He's just not easily replaceable.
I'm saying
Right now
I don't want anyone else.

IF IT'S ANY CONSOLATION

She wants to complain about how you treat her
But she doesn't want to upset you
She knows she deserves better
You are not the one
All that color she thought she'd found when you came
Has been washed out by grey
When she thinks of what makes her happy
You no longer come to mind
Everything in a matter of moments fell apart
And you didn't bat an eye
She smiles half cracked smiles for the men that deserve it
Struggling to give them her undivided attention
She's not even sure why she wanted you to stay
Leaving the door unlocked for an unhealthy return
See the monsters aren't under the bed
They aren't hiding behind closet doors
They show up in the form of people
Pretending to love you
Faking that they crave you
Hoping you never know the difference

And when they leave
The scar tissue you have to show for it
You realize isn't a scar
But a tattoo
Something you chose to stain your heart with
But if it's any consolation
You will learn how to love and what you're capable of
What you want
And what you don't
Then after you have healed
The one that patiently waited for your epiphany
Will have had the light on
As if to remind you that
Love is still the best form of magic
And anything is possible
And when this love takes its final form
He won't just show you colors
He'll paint a picture with you

YOU TO YOU

His interest is elsewhere
I feel sorry
Not for myself
For the time I wasted trying to love him
Instead of someone else
I feel bad
For the things I care about that I neglected
He pays no mind that I gave up
Because he does not care
He never cared
I get so wrapped up in what I think I want
I don't realize when it's unhealthy
I move like a bullet train to the conclusion of things
But now
I just want to slow down
I still want all the things we talked about
I just want them with someone else
They way you discuss them with someone else
He does all the things you should've
All the things you never would

I haven't opened the door for him to walk through
Because ours has to be locked tight first
But you have made it clear that you don't want this
And he has made it clear that he does
It's the pursuit of happiness
In order to get it you must pursue it
And we are standing still
I don't want you to be anywhere you don't want to be
And I am so tired of suffering in silence
Late night dates and hand holding
I am simple
And I asked for simple almost irrelevant things
Things that you couldn't do
Like don't lie and express yourself
Be loyal
Try
Like other women
I wanted so badly for you to be it that I ignored all the signs that you weren't
I'm sure you'll do all the right things for someone one day
But someone isn't me
And I
Am oddly okay with that
I'm not bitter or scorned
I look forward to doing the things I did for you
For someone who will appreciate them
Someone who will wake up at night in a panic because they think I've gone
His scent will be familiar to me after a few weeks
He will leave such an imprint on my soul that it will be as if you never existed
And when I realized that I had started to dream up these things
That this was what I was craving

Someone who would love and appreciate me
For exactly who I am
I thought of him
And I would've overlooked him
I wouldn't have went back
Unless I had been treated so poorly
So unloved
So neglected by you
Because now I know what it really means when someone doesn't care for you
Doesn't want the best for you
Doesn't want to love you
So for us this is the end
But for me this is the beginning
I know that you'll be ok
You'll survive you always do
You never appreciated what you had
So it's time for me
To leave you to you

OPTIMISM

Tell me how we're supposed to grow from this
If we can't even find where to go from this
It's like a hit and miss
All this subliminal-ness
Relentless painless tragic spins
On what this thing really is
And I'm amiss
Tell me how we're supposed to take it back February
When we were fucking different people in January
It's all a fairytale that'll never come true
A story that you'll tell your hoes too
When the liquor and drugs has got you smooth
And you want to call but you won't
And I want to shut up and listen
But I don't
So we circle around "could be "
Waiting for me to betray you while you play me
And let you
Cause somewhere I'm still holding on the fact that aftermath is in the past and we've moved on to something better than this
But we don't
We just keep playing fucked up games and now were both ashamed of where we've taken it
Shouldn't have taken it
So literal
Shouldn't gotten so physical
Now the only touch I crave is yours

But only penetrate me mentally
Stimulate simplicity make it all make sense to me
I used to fall for your every line
Now I just coast on a lost rewind
I want to go back in time
When we made promises that we thought to keep and it was all so simple to me
To give up would be a tragedy
We aren't who we thought we'd be
But let's see...
And I don't want to hurt or lie
I want to see if you'll even try
Or will you give up and let us die
Now let's see...

CHOICES

I know what moving on means.
I know it's a sign of growth.
But is missing someone
Craving someone all that bad?
Does the last chapter written really mean the story is over?
What if the pieces never fit because of it?
What if on the cold nights and warm days
All I want is you.
Poor you.
Poor me.
Poor us.
Poor what was.
Poor faith.
Poor lost hope.
Poor broken hearts.
What if when I thought I was miserable with you I was wrong?
What if I assumed there was happiness after you and I was wrong.
I thought I had had enough and I was wrong.
I thought I understood you and I was wrong.

Discovery

I should've tried harder.
I shouldn't have held my tongue.
How can you love someone so much who is so different?
Who is not perfect?
Who was so selfish?
So unappreciative?
How could you not see how much I cared?
How much effort went into you?
Why did you not care?
Why did all that effort go into you?
Why do I still give a fuck?
Knowing better.
I can see the light fading
Slipping back into the dark and I am unable to save myself.
Even though I didn't think it was that bright when you were here?
How did I fuck this up?
Did I fuck this up
Everything for reason
Treason, non-truth.
I wish I could take it all back.
To the day before I met you.
Since, I've seen the end.
How you just move along as if I never mattered.
I never mattered.
I know that now.
We both knew it then.
The state it leaves me in.
I'd take it all back.
I'd go all the way back.
Silly girl.
Don't cry.
Do not question yourself.

Question the choice
Deciding on
Loving someone you will never be able to please.

GRATEFUL FOR IT ALL: FREE WRITE

I am so grateful for the things I have realized on this last journey. I am strangely at peace with the way things are working out because I know that everything happened just the way it was supposed to. I wouldn't have found out that a fire that's meant to burn will never burn out. That it takes two people not just one draining the life from the other but each trying to give life. That people will tell you they want something that they either truly don't want or truly don't want to work for at the moment or just with you. And that, is perfectly ok. Because you need to know what love doesn't feel like. To know what it is. You need to know that you aren't selfish. That you can be faithful even when you should just move along. That you can have faith in people. This book is partly centered around a man that I had more faith in than I had in myself. More hope for him than I had for myself. I spent so much of my progression trying to progress with him that I didn't notice he didn't want to move at all. I allowed myself to be used for far longer than I should have. Deadened friendships with men that I never had reason to doubt. But throughout this process I uncovered a passion to fight for myself in a way I never even knew was possible AND the person who I have discovered in myself. I am not bitter. I do not hate people. I don't think all men are evil or not trusting of relationships. But I know that all the feelings you gave me. It reminded me of the familiar in myself. That's all it took. I was right about you being the end all to be all. You opened my eyes to my soul mate. And that is a gift I could never repay you for.

LEAVE THE DOOR UNLOCKED/3 AM

Eyes wide shut
But I'm not sleeping though
And I don't have a man
It's not like we're sneaking
So
Unlatch your belt
But do it slow
I like the show
One for you
And one for me
So high up I can barely see
Make me scream
Your name in a dark room
We don't have to talk
Let the moans say it all for us
I'll let you have your way
You'll be the hunter
I'll be the prey

I never say no
Until you want me to
Harder
Faster
Slower
Softer
I'll say that shit you like
You know
Like
Te amo papi
Pero justo hacerme cum
So go ahead
Come home from work
Slide inside
The covers
Wake me up
I'll leave the door unlocked

LAST MISTAKE

He used to put the light in the dark
Bring color to the grey
Illuminated all of my tarnished parts
Now
He's just a memory
Gone and soon forgotten
Just once I don't want it to end this way
Just once I don't want it to end
He's the nightmare not even S.King could dream up
He's hell in an already war-torn place
He's the night after Katrina
The empty desolate place where the last piece of my heart broke
The bomb that went off right after my soul died out
He was my last mistake

HOPEFUL

What if it's all a dream he says
I mean what if we wake up one day and it's over
I don't live by 'what if' I live by what is
I thought about it though for a second
Like what if we never had really held hands by the ocean
What if we had never fallen apart the first 6 times we had tried to fall together
What if the white picket fence
The 4 bedroom 2.5 bathroom
Two car garage is an illusion
Then it dawned on me that I wanted something deeper
So I asked him
What if we could count the stars
What if nothing was impossible
If we were the revolution
If nothing was infinite and everything was defined
We knew there was no purple matter
Or other galaxies out there
That we were it
We were all that was created
He frowned
He looked as if his world, the Fabergé egg that it always was
Was shattered into tiny pieces
Then what would we have to believe in
I smiled I kissed him
Transferring my energy to him
See I whispered
Hope

BLUE SKIES

Wish I could rewind
Replace you with the new
What I wouldn't give to be stretched across the couch
My feet in your lap
While you draw up some old school west coast Santeria
While I write new poetry and song lyrics
Music playing in background
I just miss talking to you
About
Political views, take over and conspiracies
How the universe is bigger than we ever could even imagine
And
About how our souls are connected eternally
How 11:11 wasn't just a theory
How you and I were 3rd world memories
I remember telling you not to worry
And you saying
How you'll never be good enough
How I'm worth so much more than this
Five years later and the smell of you still lingers
Stale
In that old sweat shirt
When you go to war with the one person you care the most for
It breaks you
Even long after the waters are calm and your spirits move on

Discovery

Remember back when you were just some kid across the cafeteria
And when you'd just ride past my house 'til my step dad was gone
And all our fights ended with
"No matter I'll never leave you alone"
Out of all the promises you couldn't keep
That one is the one that gets to me
They wear your name on T-Shirts that end in R.I.P
That shit is so tacky to me
And all these old videos are haunting to me
I can hear you when I'm sober
And it's frightening to me
To think
That everything we ever talked about will
Never be
You are up there
And I am down here
But you're sheltering me
Two different places
How it always seems to be
If I just fall asleep the way you did
You think then you could come rescue me
You think if I don't get it together you'll be the death of me
Black knights
Blue skies
Pink matter
Orange dreams
Still means something to me

CHARLIE

New love
With that old school feel
Vibing on another level
Swearing it's real
Bitter enough to leave a bad taste in your mouth
Curious enough to see what your about
And yet
Nothing ever came of this
Like summer love and winter storms
You came
And went
Drunk mumbling your old rap lyrics
I swear I'm tired of it
I just want to shake the feeling
That you were as real as it'll ever get
I'm still alive
But haven't lived yet
Crossovers
Elevation
Higher levels of self
Late night creative cravings
That I'll never get a fix to
Pieces I don't get back
Because you took them all with you

DISCOVERY

I recently wrote a series of poems.
That I was struggling with the decision to publish.
If I'm being honest and with the poetry I always am
Out of shame.
And then I remembered.
Art. Poetry.
It's how I heal.
Like some wounded animal.
This is how I lick my wounds.
I told myself that I
Would stop allowing my heart to get me into situations that my mind just can't get me out of.
I promised myself that the last time was the last time.
I don't blame anyone else.
I know that this is all my fault.
I seek out self destruction the way an addict needs a fix.
Love has never been the heroine.
It has always been the heartbreak.
See when you are truly addicted to pain.
You find a way to get it.
Just maybe this time I took too much.
Maybe this once I over did it.
I have taken the last of what I had left.
And tore it.
Into a million little pieces

NIGHT FALLS

Being with you was like seeing the city at night for the first time
All lit up and beautiful
Loud and crazy
Wild how the sky never lights the same in the sunshine
Guess the sun and the moon have different points of view
Our own shadows disappear leaving us to fend for ourselves
While everyone watches
And I can't seem to open up my third eye long enough to grasp what your trying to say
But it sounds a lot like hopeful regrets about needing to walk away
And I want to leave you too
But just as I reach for my shoes
The sun comes up
And you see me
And that light
That shadow that got cast away when the night came
Woke up with a lot to say
So I just drift to the sound of your heartbeat
Til the sunshine goes away

A POEM FOR JOSEPH

I thought I knew what life was
I figured the never ending cycle of disappointment and
heartbreak was just how it was supposed to go
That nothing was forever
That while I spoke of it
It would never be possible to love in permanent ink
Then I met you
And I understood what missing someone really meant
Because you were gone after the introduction
I knew after you touched me
That no touch would ever feel the same
And that yours was worth the wait
That constant reminder when you look at me
That it's ok to be lost in another person
That no matter where this ends up
I could never place this again
That now that my circle has been completed
Now everything makes sense
That notion that
Somethings are just worth holding on to
Immediately after I met you
I understood what it was like to want everything and nothing
At the same time
I knew that every love poem
I had ever written was about you

Every sweet song I had ever learned the words to were for you
That you gave a dreamer something new to dream about
And that with you
All possibilities
Are endless

THE BOY

I met this boy
She chimed
He seems pretty perfect
He causes that tingle in my hands
Twitch in my toes
He's like the favorite movie you just can't get enough of
And his kisses are among the best I've ever tasted
And...
She's rambling
She stops
Your laughter is boisterous and too much to take
Why are you laughing
I'm being serious
Straight facing her delusions of grandeur
You speak slowly as to not cut too deeply into the flesh
While trying to remove the infection
And you say
Child
Beautiful smart thing
There lays the problem
You.
Met.
A.
Boy.
A boy will keep you dreaming
A man will make you grow
A king will make you a queen
And when you really find him.
You.
Will.

Know.
The difference.
She frowned.
That feeling.
Though it may be as temporary as you say
Is a feeling I would gladly feel over and over again.
And if only men make you grow.
Then what is the purpose behind a woman.
If only Kings make Queens
Then where do Kings come from
Who really ever knows.
What if this is all there was ever meant to be.
What if
Boy vs Man
Woman vs Man
Queen Vs King and vice versa isn't good enough?
....

MENTAL DISORDER

I'm always competition and never the partner
The thing you run away from
Not toward
The scary misunderstood abstract art
The tool you never use the right way
I know this is because
I leave random little love notes on schizophrenic paper
That I leave as gifts
Wrapped up in bipolar disorder
Leaving you to find them
Like a mad hatter in Wonderland
And I know that makes no sense
But it's perfectly put together for me
I am trying to show you love
In the most dysfunctional of ways
Because I am not quite sure how to tell you
That you are the most sane thing to ever happen to me
That if you were to ever leave
The pieces of the puzzle
That never fit in the first place
Will dissolve into sand
And as crazy as that sounds
It happens more often than I'd like to realize
But If I am sand
Then that makes you the ocean
Standing til we sink
And I know it sounds like rambling
I know it makes no sense
But love never does
I think

Bianca Sanders

MOVEMENT

I like who I turned out to be
So can you please stop pestering me
Telling me how I've changed
How you wanted me to stay the same
Hindering me
I'm right where I'm supposed to be
Elevated to higher level, showing me
Slowing me
Down
As if I'd never get off the ground
I'm going to show you now
What 'The Movement' was all about

ART TO ANOTHER ARTIST

Can't you just come over
Crawl in the bed how you used to
So we can do what I'm used to
What I only want with you
Remember the days
You kept your things at my place
And I trusted you to keep the things I was made of safe
When we talked about new tattoos and good music
When you would take one hand and run it over my thighs
Bury your face in my hair
Plant kisses down my neck
Boy I drink up those memories like a good   chardonnay
When you told me you knew we'd last
Because I didn't judge your past
When you said you were comfortable with dating another artist
When we split
I swore to never do it again
But I'm laying here reading messages from what has to be two years ago
Defying time by asking
Where the time has flown
Rest your hand between my legs
With my head on your chest

Discovery

"You vs Them" playing through the speaker
You don't ask what happened with him
I don't care what happened to her
They were fillers for this
Listen I just want to show you what you've been missing
Kissing touching to fuckin
Wet dreams
Only
This
Is the real thing
I just want to be your last stroke of genius
Your favorite kind of paint
The piece you'll never quite be done with
You can be the poem I never write about
The one I never read out loud
The one I keep to myself
Something so familiar
That I read when I start missing you
When I get lonely
You mix me with your blues and yellows
And grip my canvas with your mouth
And drain the soul out of me
You will always be my favorite piece

REMINISCE

Called your old number tonight.
I knew you wouldn't answer
It's not your number anymore
I tried replacing you with a replacement that didn't fit the bill
I tried to right my wrongs from 4 years ago in someone new
Someone who wasn't you
Instead of binging on my favorite book
Tonight I'll watch our old videos and read our messages
I think I even kept the letters written on that ugly ass yellow paper.
 And the drawings you sent from
 Anyway
 Te amo papi descansa en paz
 Pero cuando llegue allí estamos   terminando nuestra partida de ajedrez

STILL

A CO told me 5 months ago:
Don't ever put your life on hold for anyone.
It's not going to be how you think it will be.
I can tell you've got a lot going for you.
You need to prepare for what happens when and if they have the   opportunity to show you and they fail/disappoint you.
People have demons they won't tell you about.
Do your research.
The fact is if they are the one they won't hold you back
I promise.
Best advice I was ever given.
I knew it all stuck by my choice
And now I have no regrets no "what ifs"
Just countless blessings.
Everything for a <u>reason</u>
<u>It</u> did not fail.
It changed me for the better.
I did everything for a reason.

But the reality of the situation is
I will always want him and we did fail.
That is the only regret.

LOST

I was caught up in the way that he made me feel
In my own turmoil
Then I remembered the day you laid in my bed and told me that
You are more sensitive than I knew
And I remember not believing you
I remember thinking it was some sort of ploy So that I wouldn't see you as the villain
Even though you never really were
I remember being confused as to why you said it
Now the only thing I realize
The one thing that matters
Is that you were telling the truth
That you never wanted to complicate things
That you were honest
Yet I
In my own impatience and lack of understanding went elsewhere
When I should've stayed
Went to someone who caused far more damage than you could imagine
And now
Alone in that same bed I think
I wonder how many other women
Have failed to hear your honesty and speak to your truth
How many others have only touched your surface
How many others failed to realize that you are so much deeper than this

I pray that I was the last
I apologize for my neglect
Because now I understand what it feels like
To be listened to and not heard

A POEM TO MY BOYS

Zephaniah and Zechariah
The best thing I've ever done
The only thing
I've ever really done
Was be their mother
And 97% of the time I wonder if I am doing it right
3% of the time I know for sure I am failing
But they have managed to bring light to my dark places
To be gifts when I don't deserve to be gifted
To give so much love and life to such as lifeless place
That I actually understood how a rose grew from concrete
They are the God Kings of my mythological   story
The beginnings that show no sign of end
Tangible
They are perfect things.
My best forms of creation
Proof that I in fact can work with other artist
People of perfection
And forever
My boys

WHERE TO

I did not get to pick him.
It was not a choice.
Just the free will to decide whether or not to stay.
The fact of the matter is
He was and will always be the one I always wanted.
The one that even though we are so vastly complicated he is the only thing that will ever matter again.
The one where if the ending is anything different than you will never quite be good enough.
And that is where the real complication came from.
Because in two motions
You gave all hope and then took it all away.
Leaving me with nothing to turn to.
I have no idea what's next.

15 IS NOT ENOUGH

Sometimes
I just can't get all the words out
I'm often like that
Not knowing what to say
Strange quality in a writer
But it's just
It's like
I have a million things I want to say to you at once
But I can't
I can't because you can't fit a million things in 15 minutes
I can't because I don't want to annoy you
I can't because if I tell you all one million things then I won't hear your one million things
I want to tell you everything I did today
And last year
And the year before that
I want to tell you all the bad things
But remind you of the good
I want to know if you're as emotional as I am
Do you get anxious too
Do you ever feel lost in your own familiar
Do people think you're crazy?
Are you crazy
I want to know what your heartbeat sounds like when you're nervous
Did I ever make you nervous?
I have a million questions

I want to know everything about you
Even the parts that you don't know yet
Like were you ever afraid of the dark?
Like do you want more children
How good are you at chess
Do you want a family
What's your stance on dishwashing
Who would do the laundry
If I'm upset and you can't fix it
Will you sit with me in silence until I feel better
A million things I need to know
Even more that I want to say
But we only have 15 minutes
Today.
I hope there's more time

LITTLE THINGS

You aren't like the others
You came at a strange time
In a moment when I was in complete peace
You brought in a calming chaos
I noticed little things about you
How you're stand offish and stubborn
You're sincerely sweet
You don't scream attention
But you do enough to be noticed
These are just the little things
As time passed I notice you're so patient
It seems as if you don't care at all
That you reek of adolescence
I got a sense of you when I realized that when we fight you never try to hurt me
That it seems as if it's me hurting you
That maybe there are two villains in this story
I compensate by reminding myself how bad you hurt me
How you left scars deeper than C-sections birthing lifeless bodies into the world
That you are the storm that has no calm after it
You are the permanent damage I begged for
Received at the worst time
You are more effective than black coffee after an all-nighter
Yeah
I notice the little things

I NEVER

I Never kiss a boy
With my eyes closed in the moonlight of deep conversation
I Never kiss a boy
After an emotional day when my whole world has fallen apart
With the expectation that he will make it whole again
I Never kiss a boy in a car
In the dead of winter
Too high to know better
I Never kiss a boy
Who grips my thigh on the highway while he lip syncs silly song lyrics
Unless
Of course
He's you
I'll never understand what happened to us
I'll never stop wanting it back

JUST WAITING

I wake up most days in a panic
I realize you just aren't here
I can't wait for those days to be over
For the darkness to end
For only the light to shine in
Countless amounts of poetry and you still aren't here
I wonder when you get here
How long it will take before you leave
I hope it takes a while
Because living in the moment is never quite enough
Because I know that the recovery from you will be endless
I wonder if you know how perfectly imperfect and amazing I see you
I wonder if you notice
That I don't see anything greater than this...

SOBERING

Ever wonder why they show you so much love when it's over
Because love is easier said than done
...
Don't mind me...
I'm just thinking...
Sober

....
And I can never get just high enough to forget how I felt about you
Never quite sober enough to somber
You turned out to be more like cotton candy than taffy
At the sign of a light mist you dissipate
Leaving behind sticky fingerprints
All over me as if to let the men that will come after you know that you were here
Why couldn't you
Just this once clean up after yourself
I can't let anyone get close to me now
I don't want them to see that I am a mess
I don't want them to find me crying aimlessly
Stumbling over, getting over you
In a dimly lit parking lot cursing the idea of us
Trying to figure out which parts weren't real
Did you ever plan to drive the whole 17 hours

....
Don't mind me....
I'm just up thinking.....
Sober.....

START OVER

College starts in the fall
And to think she thought she knew it all
She blew it all
Because she blew them all
Off
No time
And now there is no one left
I guess she just needed to know she was   the best
Put all those daddy issues to rest
Laid his head on her chest
And told her his secrets
Guess because the timing is off
In another lifetime
This still would've been bullshit
Guess she thought it would be something you'd be cool with
She was wrong
And so was he
Let it go
Let it be

FINAL EXPLANATION

I never really could explain how I felt about you when I was with you
I'm almost famous for that
It's like all the feeling is there but I do not have the words
When it's over it is the exact opposite
I can give you full details about how much I loved you
Now
That the feeling is gone
I can tell you how
Touching you're for the first time felt like warming up next to a bon fire at the first change of fall
How you
Are like a deep breath during an asthma attack
How meeting you face to face for the first time
Felt like the first day of high school
I could tell you that
You
Gave my soul chills
Like the way your body just senses that seasons have shifted
I can now explain how
You
Make me feel the way I felt giving my first speech in 3rd grade
Nervous but confident
You make all of hair on the back of my neck stand up
Because even when you are nowhere around me
I feel your energy move through my body

Discovery

Like a drug
I can tell you that you are my addiction
That my body will still feel the effects of you in my bones
Long after the connection subsides
How I'll want you
Forever
The way people miss summer during a winter snow storm
Wondering why it never could stay

FEEL

If I close my eyes I can remember the smallest details about you
From how your hands feel
How your eyes tell a story you never told
I can almost pick up on your disappointments
And sometimes when you speak
I can hear the fear in your voice
The uncertainty your past brought with it
I want to tell you I understand
But I don't think you'd believe me
I want to tell you how I feel
But I don't know if you will trust it
Because I know that most people measure in time not feeling
So you won't quite understand when I tell you that
You
Have penetrated my inner most thoughts
That the idea of you is what's at the end of all the rainbows
That everything we talk about is a promise I make to not give up until you do
And should the day ever come where I am not enough
Where you wonder if you are enough
When you doubt yourself
When you wonder whether or not you can keep up with words that have been spoken
When you can't seem to decide if the right foundation was laid
I'll stand next to you
Hold your hand and remind you that the depth of your voice alone is enough to change lives
That you are the warrior you never saw in the mirror
That the battles you fight within yourself you don't have to go at

alone.
I will be the subtle reminder that
While it's easier to go than it is to stay
Staying is where you find purpose
That you don't give yourself enough credit
You are stronger than what you think.
But I also know you can't force things like this.
That as uneven and unpaved as the road is
You have what it takes to carve us out the right path
That I stand beside you
Because I believe in you
That you.
Make me feel everything.
And if I can only give one thing back to the world.
If I could only make one person see one thing.
Give one gift outside of my children
It wouldn't hesitate to sacrifice myself.
I wouldn't cower to commit or submit.
Without considering the repercussions.
I would give that to you.
The ability to feel.
To know your worth.
To honor your greatness beyond the superficial.
Because I have seen into the depths beyond the surface.
And I know how great you can be
I know just how influential you are

LONG WALK

And the best thing about him
She held her breath
Was knowing that I could bare my soul at every poetry showcase
And not worry about his reaction from the front row
Even better
She noted
I don't have to be there when he reads the poetry that is about him
I will never have to cringe at knowing that he never read the pages that were written for him
I hope he is at peace
I hope he finds happiness
I will always speak highly of him
Even when he had made me feel at my lowest
I will embrace the breaking point
The adventure that was him
Because it elevated me to a higher level of being
I realized that the goons in dark alleyways
Live in my mind
That my instinct will never betray me
Even though often people do
That trust isn't something you should just give away
And to always save the brightest pieces of yourself
For something more permanent
Always guard yourself freely
Be open but don't touch
And if you ever have to wonder if you're good enough

Walk away
But walk peacefully
Walk soft don't disturb his peace when you leave
And don't take their demons with you
Just knowing that you loved him was enough
And that his reaction to it is irrelevant
Because it was your decision
Your choice
Walk for as long as you need to

IN TIME

It's crazy how much you care about someone
Who you never thought you would
When all of your "I's" become "we's"
Good or bad, better or worse
You stay when your first instinct should be to go
Something keeps your feet grounded in the same spot
When you know you're great at running away
Your heart makes you stay
Lover's turn into friends who fall in love quick
At a time you least expect it
In a moment you thought was all wrong
It feels like insanity
Like a gravitational pull that swept you up in a right direction
At the highest speed imaginable
Nothing happens at the wrong time
Love isn't tangible
I didn't understand that until this
I didn't understand the difference between 'love' the verb
And 'love' the noun
They are not the same
We are not the same
Just
Similar
And yet we couldn't be more attached
And I know I speak of not belonging
But the pieces of our puzzle are so different yet create the perfect abstract picture
You are the light at the end of the tunnel

Discovery

The birdsong and sunrise
The first full moon in a new town
Before you everything was foggy
I knew the general direction
But had no real destination
You are the inamorato to my poetry
I am the inamorata to your life
Hopelessly devoting every waking minute to a change
For a future that seems so clear
On the path never traveled
Something different
Something evident
Something just like you
Now we are in a world of the found
Together
True love is never easy
Introductions were in order
The universe knew it was
Time

MORE THAN THIS

You're not better than the next
Stressed
Watching distress
Somewhere along the way I got lost
I ended up reinventing myself for the
Hundredth time
Trying to piece it all together
But the pieces fit like porcelain plates on marble floors
What am I fighting for
I can't remember
So forgotten
In the midst of a late night and prayer
Taming lions that are not mine to train
Molding minds that I use to yield to
What am I fighting for
Memories and destiny
Speaking volumes saying nothing
While most say everything that's trifle
A little too familiar with disappearing acts
Drowning out the disappointment because most days
I'd rather be invisible anyway
You got too close
And now you know
What I know
Loss
Lost
Losing...

CONVERSATIONS WITH LOIS

"Tell me how you feel today"
I don't respond for a minute because I don't know the answer
I hate these test
I never pass them
"I don't know",
It's the truth
But I know by now not to tell the truth
I know when I give the wrong answers because she always writes those down
"Tell me about your father"
She folds her hands around her lap
She almost looks genuinely interested
"Not much to say. I don't know him really and I would like to keep it that way. My step father was an asshole and he's really not worth mentioning."
She pulls out her notebook.
"How about your boyfriend? How do you think he feels about you?"
I tell the truth
"Sometimes I am convenient and sometimes I am not. I don't think he feels anything for me beyond that and I don't blame him."
Her pen is blue.
It's his favorite color
She hits the top.
It clicks.
She asks a series of more questions and then she says
"Ok, and you? How do you feel today? I know you say you

don't know, but if you had to describe it would you say you are happy or sad, do you feel..."
She pauses
I know this pause
She's searching for a que
A blink, a twitch, anticipation that this will be the word to describe it
"....upset."
She waits
I sit perfectly still
" I am always upset and never upset. I don't really know what that means. I am just here. Same as yesterday."
She starts to write again
"Would you say you are more up than down? Or more down than up?"
She's peering over her glasses and she is studying me.
I hate this.
"My downs are upstands my ups are downs. And I can never find the middle. I either stay up too long or come down to quick. Or stay down too far and come up to slow. But either way I can never tell the difference."
She writing again
She is the mechanic of my mind.
The one they call when you can't quite help yourself
She is trying to find my broken parts so she can replace them
I am clock that she believes she can get to tell time again.
I wish I could help her get past my paranoia of broken dials but I can't.
"What I really mean to say is
I can't feel love.
I can't tell when I have it and when I don't because I don't know it.
I can't feel happiness.

Discovery

But I know what laughter sounds like and I have felt the tingle behind it and it never last longer than a few seconds.
It's blunt and mute and I can never quite feel it the way I have seen other people feel it.
But I imagine something close to it and most days that's enough.
I understand what jealousy and rage feel like. But if anger is a secondary emotion then why do I always feel it first?
I know lonely.
I know what it feels like to have your body go cold and numb from isolation and feel hollow inside.
I know how it feels to stop breathing.
But if death is wrong why do feel more alive before I want to die?"
She stares at me
She's writing
I know those are the wrong questions
But I don't think she has the answers anyway and I know I shouldn't have asked
She writes out the prescriptions
900mgs of Seroquel, celexa 40 mgs, 90 day supply
She thinks I'm crazy
She's not alone
She's probably right
She hands me the slip of tacky blue paper
This didn't help
This doesn't seem to be helping
I should stop coming
She thinks this is working
She blames the disorder
I don't know who to blame
This is all about the problem
But how can you offer a solution when you're not quite sure

what the problem is?
"That's all the time for today."
She says.
"See you next week."
I gather my bag.
I fold the prescription
She doesn't know what to do with me
I think it bothers her
I want to tell her she shouldn't let it get to her.
That it's just me.
That the tacky blue slips of paper are as close as she'll come to a resolution.
But she's already disappointed.
I'll save it for next week.

PENETRATION

We speak the same language
We just translate differently
We have to have some common ground
When she said deeper
What did you think she meant
There's got to be more to it than this
More than what you both seem to be reaching for
When he asked you to touch him
What did you think he meant
Just something different
Something
Real.

SOMETIME-Y

Sometimes I wish I could see the bad in you
Like you and the rest of the world do
Sometimes I wish I could tell you it's ok
To your face
So that you could see and read the look on mine
Sometimes I want to tell you that when I look at you
I can tell you don't think you're enough
Sometimes, I want to tell you that you are wrong
Sometimes I want to be the person you crave
Sometimes I'm glad you give me space
And when I think of how insanely horribly terrifically awful it feels to want you
I smile to myself that kind of secret smile that no one knows the reason behind
I sometimes sit and think, while waiting for you to call,
What if I had never met you
It's the saddest thought I've had in a while
Seems like such an empty life
Sometimes I believe you can't help who you love
I can't help that feeling I got the first time you made me laugh
That you
You deserve all the love and affection that one person could gather
I know I never told you
But I don't think I could imagine someone NOT loving you
I wanted to
This situation is not ideal
I would've never placed myself here years ago
But now that I know you

Discovery

I couldn't see myself going back to being alone
Because once you felt what whole feels like
Why would you want to go back to being anything else
I wish that sometimes, no all the time
Every time
Was enough

WORDS THAT LOST THE MEANING

Never listen to what they tell you,
The noise is just to create the confusion,
The delusion that you might matter,
Always hear what they mean in what they show you,
Because the noise will speak volumes,
It will pull on your delusions and taint you with your dreams,
And mean nothing,
But the actions,
They will always speak louder than words,
This,
What I have allowed,
So she stopped speaking what she craved into existence,
And let the last bit she had die out,
Nothing and no one was worth it,
The last words she spoke,
While few,
Gave it all away,
She says,
"I don't know how, or when I got to be so weak.
But the strength doesn't come on its own."

HABITS

They say
It takes twice as long to break a habit as it took to create
If that's true then, in theory,
This should not take long to get over
I wonder what sort of scar you'll leave behind
How negative of me to think that
But you're just too good to be true
Baring all your imperfections for me to see
I take you just as you are
While, the cut was quicker the wound itself will be deep
I know that this scar won't be like the rest
I won't be able to just
Bandage it
I could suture it myself
But it will just open itself up later
When I am happy with someone new
Trying to cover the mark you leave
And while I will have to let someone come to the rescue
And nurse me back to health
I'll never really recover
I'll try to forget
I'll know I'm better after the fire dies down and the knives aren't being wielded
Probably around the same time you start to love your ex
The girl you "never dated" to begin with
And even knowing all of this

I will never really recover
They say
It takes twice as long to break a habit as it takes to create it
I don't know who they are
But they
Are wrong
Hopefully, though
When you get home
This won't be a concern
Just a paranoid poem
From a hopeless romantic
Who fell for someone so perfectly different
That you become the last habit I ever form

MORE THAN I CAN BARE

I keep looking back trying to figure out what I did wrong
Where I went wrong
I try to come to reason with the realization that this is really happening
That this really happened
I want to try and focus on the positives in my life
I keep telling myself that if you can be happy
So can I
I keep trying to figure out how it is so easy for you
But I don't want to think about that at all
I went from never dreaming to having nightmares every night
Of you in there
Me out here
You make it sound so horrible
It probably really is
Even still
I would gladly trade you places so you didn't have to go through that hell
Got me questioning the Higher Power
I thought God never gave you more than you could bare

NEVER AGAIN

We hurt and heal differently. But love all the same.

Put your whole heart into it
Because inevitability it will change
Grow and evolve
Into one direction or another
How can she say she wants you whole heartedly
And not take you whole
Who you are, were, becoming as if she didn't know what she signed up for
Two wanders find each other in the strangest of places
You aren't wrong but neither is she
Finding a balance is key
But she's cloaking you in the darkness that she has surrounded herself in
She doesn't mean to
She makes just as many mistakes as you do
She is not a victim
She is just as much to blame
She is unsure of almost everything
But she knows that you are where she wants to be
The raw energy is enough to hold on to
Sink your teeth into her
Let her sink her claws into you
She's scared too
She wonders what happens if this relationship fails
She wonders what happens if it doesn't
Both equally terrifying
Stay together
Fall together
Never to fall apart again

SKIN ON SKIN

So, She says
Come lay with me for a minute
He reasons
Why?
You're mad
This is the worst time to be next to you
She's in pain
He knows he hurt her
He wants to fix it why else would he be here
She wants to fix it why else would she be here
You couldn't be more wrong
This is when I need to lay next to you the most
Because if I can't feel it your words
And can't read it in your body language
Then I need to feel it in your energy
Skin on skin
Instead let's just do it like we never did it the first time
Like there were no mistakes
Start over selflessly
The beginnings are always the best

DOING IT WRONG

I don't know if I want to hurt you because
I want you to know what it feels like to
Not be able to put a Band-Aid on the scars that are left and carry on
Or
If it's because that is the only way I have been programmed to detach
By ripping into you like claws from a wild rabbit
Stripping the surface wounds open
Maybe I am secretly hoping
That if I can get you to hate me
Then I can move on safely
Pretending that I never loved you at all
But I would only be putting on a show
A façade
Because I did
And I never wanted to hurt you
But then again
I never thought I would have to save myself from you either
When he is used to temporary
Give him something permanent
If he doesn't value it
Then let him continue to search for what he is looking for in peace
It doesn't mean he's wrong
He will prove to had been good practice
You're "temporary "
Eventually, after he has gone
You're permanent
Your reason
Will come along and you will understand why he couldn't stay

THE LONGEST WAIT EVER

My palms sweat
My brain tries to make sense of a senseless situation
It's a pull on two worlds that somehow collided to form something,
Something different,
Something whole
To have your brain take you to a place that your heart never meant to go
To have another person take this world of chaos you've lived in and make it slow down
Have you doing things you didn't even know where possible
This something, it makes you realize that you can't go back,
That you could never go back even if you could,
Even if you wanted to,
That the touch of their hand,
That look that they give you,
That thing you couldn't let go of,
That selfishness that you held onto,
It can't live here,
In this place,
For the first time,
You know what it's like to choose someone else,
And maybe in retrospect this is ultimately how you chose yourself,
This is how you love yourself,
Worlds apart and different in every aspect,
Yet, still somehow it makes sense
You realize it doesn't take two worlds.
Just two people trying to make one world work
I almost want to cry

But I don't cry
All this effort
All for nothing
All for something
Hopes higher than air balloons
Maybe I overthink things
Maybe that's why I'm alone
Maybe that's why I never work
You lived in me before I knew you existed
I know I deserve better
I know you expected something different
I know I move at a different pace and this is something different
The feeling is different
Run it through the rinse cycle
Two hearts washed clean
Like glass shattered on pavement
We were an accident
One that was meant to happen
A moment of impact
And no matter how it turns out
I'm glad it existed
I think about this while I wait
To talk to you without touching
10 am on Sunday
The ideas are always this deep
On visiting day

THE COUNT OF MONTE CRISTO

An old flame once told me that some flames end the way the Count and Mercedes did. That even though they loved each other.
Too much damage had been done.
That he would never fight for her the way he wanted to.
That it would be easier for him to move on. Since, everything in the Counts life was already so difficult he would leave her, knowing how deeply she loved him, and how much she would sacrifice to be with him.
Because he had gone through so much to find himself after her that he couldn't go back.
Maybe out of fear that she would never love him quite the same.
Or that he would ever love her quite the same.
Either way, I didn't buy it.
I mean after all love conquers all things.
Endures all things.
His view point was for quitters and people that didn't believe in "happily ever after".
But then I met you.
I watched our fire burn out before it had even really started.
I saw you go off to something else, somewhere else, with someone else.
And I realized.
 I am very much Mercedes and you are very much the Count.

THE LETTER

I believe that everything happens for a reason. EVERYTHING. I sent this letter to someone I cared about once. He never got it. A short time later, we ended. I found the saved copy of the letter. The one I never attempted to resend and merged it with some emails I never sent him. This is not a poem. Just letters that were never opened.

Maybe you're right. I think too much. I worry too much, or not enough. It's hard to tell which anymore. My greatest fear is not that I will ever regret the choice to be with you or the decision I will eventually make to love you day after day. My greatest fear, is that one day the beauty you see in me will fade, and the light around me will grow dark and you will stop caring about me. That the compassion will dry out. I have nightmares about someone else touching you, loving you. Someone else laying next to you. That someone else will know the rhythm of your heartbeat better than I do. And that you will know hers. That she will be the one to place kisses down your neck. And hold your hand through the stormy days. To cuddle up to you on cold nights.my ultimate fear is that this love, all the while eternal, won't last us through this lifetime. And that, is a devastation I couldn't survive. I hate that we fought today. I hate that it was my fault. I'm sorry.
I would be willing to do anything to make this right if knew for sure it were the right thing. I don't know which one of us owns a greater share of the blame. But I do know that neither of those things matter now. We are both hurt. We are both scared. And now, sober from a harsh reality and exhausted from hours of

tears, I want to be connected more than I want to be right. I can see my mistakes. I usually can, after the smoke clears. I want you to know, I'm sorry. I usually am after the smoke clears. But I'm afraid to tell you that. I'm afraid that if I admit my mistakes. Afraid that you'll use them against me. I'm afraid you'll think acknowledging my mistakes means you will not be responsible for acknowledging yours. I'm afraid of being the woman who lets you off the hook, the woman who settles for less than your best. Especially when, I have more faith in you than I, most days, have in myself. I try and want to be the woman who sees the quality of what we're capable of cultivating, knows that it requires tremendous courage and work and believes so unwaveringly in your ability to show up for it that she accepts nothing less. In that same notion, somehow trying to be encouraging and patient without complaining. But I am not perfect. And I have not figured it all out, but I am, trying. I push and push to make sure you hear my side, to make sure you understand what I'm asking of you. When I'm not sure that you've heard me, understood me. But I am trying to listen to you too. I am trying to give you what you need not just physically or financially but emotionally, spiritually and mentally. I am trying to figure out how to do that. How to take a risk without losing. But I guess that's how you lose. I tell you to make a choice. The greatest fear is not knowing what you'll choose. I can go at least another 12 rounds because the idea of giving up on you is not at all what I want to do. But I'll leave it up to you.
-B

------He didn't stay. I can't say I blame him. I'm not sure what would've happened if he would've. I pitched a theory on twin flames two weeks before I met him. The theory on twin flames(in case you didn't know) is that two people who are usually polar opposites and not a typical pair. Are pushed together by the universe. That even in the worlds outside of this one their souls know each other. They are together or, at the very least, have crossed paths. They will leave an impression on each other once they have met that will allow them to recognize each other when their souls move on to other worlds. An impression that can never be mimicked. Whether they are together for a few days, months or years, doesn't matter because the connection is that strong. One of the stages of 'The Twin Flame Cycle' states that eventually they will be separated. For whatever reason and quite possibly more than once or in more than one way; and maybe they come back together in this life, in this world, maybe they don't, but nothing after that will feel the same. Nothing after that will feel like it's good enough.

Discovery

ABOUT THE AUTHOR

Bianca Sanders has been writing since she was 13. She has predominately written poetry and short stories. She is expanding to writing children's books, novels and novellas. She currently lives in Kentucky with her family.

www.ingramcontent.com/pod-product-compliance
Lightning Source LLC
Chambersburg PA
CBHW032020040426
42448CB00006B/676